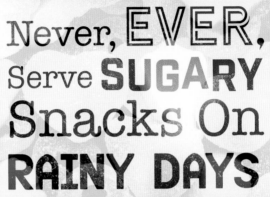

Never, EVER, Serve SUGARY Snacks On RAINY DAYS

and Other Words of Wisdom for
Teachers of Young Children

Shirley R.

Gryphon House

www.gryphonhouse.com

Bulk Purchase
Gryphon House books are available for special premiums and sales promotions as well as for fund-raising use. Special editions or book excerpts also can be created to specifications. For details, call 800.638.0928.

Disclaimer
Gryphon House, Inc., cannot be held responsible for damage, mishap, or injury incurred during the use of or because of activities in this book. Appropriate and reasonable caution and adult supervision of children involved in activities and corresponding to the age and capability of each child involved are recommended at all times. Do not leave children unattended at any time. Observe safety and caution at all times.

Dear Readers,

Several years ago, my niece decided she wanted to become a teacher. She made the mistake of asking me, a former teacher, for advice. Out of my tips for her came my first advice book: *Never, EVER, Serve Sugary Snacks on Rainy Days: The Official Little Instruction Book for Teachers of Young Children*. Since that time, I have served education in many capacities. I have published research articles that have won awards and written successful books about using children's literature in the curriculum.

Now, as a speaker at early childhood conferences and at leadership-development sessions, audience members often mention my little advice book, which they usually call *Never, Ever*. Their continued interest prompted me to update the book. It is dedicated to those audience members, to my niece, and to the extraordinary students I have known who have become extraordinary teachers. Like the original, the new edition is filled with humor, common sense, admonitions, and silly and serious advice.

My best advice remains: Let the children be children, and trust yourself and your quality education that has prepared you to become the teacher you are.

Yours truly,
Shirley Raines

Shirley's grandchildren, Riley Marie and Bryson Smith

Wear sunglasses outside,
so you can pretend not to see everything
that happens on the playground.

IGNORE THUMB
SUCKING—
UNLESS IT'S
SOMEONE ELSE'S
THUMB.

Invite musicians, artists, and dancers to your class.

And celebrate all children as musicians, artists, and dancers.

Dream a lot.
Dream what the children in your classroom can become.

"Splish" and "splash" are children's favorite sounds.

Yellow umbrellas
are great props,
even on sunny days.

KEEP PEACE BY MAKING SURE EVERYONE HAS A PIECE OF THE ACTION.

Taking turns on riding toys requires serious and skillful negotiations.

Creativity happens all day, not just during music and art classes.

Beg for art supplies. Directors always buy art supplies. But make sure the supplies go to your classroom, not just to the art teacher who sees the children once a week.

Gender equity means
boys need to cook
and girls need to hammer,
and girls need to cook
and boys need to hammer.

*Watch for early signs of spring
and for signs of late bloomers.*

Count fingers, toes, and noses—not mistakes.

LEARN A FEW WORDS IN EVERY LANGUAGE SPOKEN BY THE CHILDREN.

Remember, dialects are beautiful.

Get back to the basics: sing, dance, tell a story.

Learn a new fingerplay each month.

Sing or chant the new fingerplay in at least one other language, even if you have no non-English speakers in your class.

Music brings the class together, quiets the room, and steadies a teacher's nerves.

NEVER, EVER, ASK THE CHILDREN WHAT THEY WANT TO SING . . .

UNLESS YOU ARE PREPARED TO SING "JINGLE BELLS" IN JULY, "FIVE LITTLE JACK-O'-LANTERNS" IN APRIL, AND "YANKEE DOODLE DANDY" IN OCTOBER.

Always have a song
in your heart . . .

and one of the children's favorite songs ready to play in an instant.

When the curriculum isn't emerging well, like you thought it would, plan a merging curriculum.

Merge the children's interests and some lesson plans you can get together in a hurry.

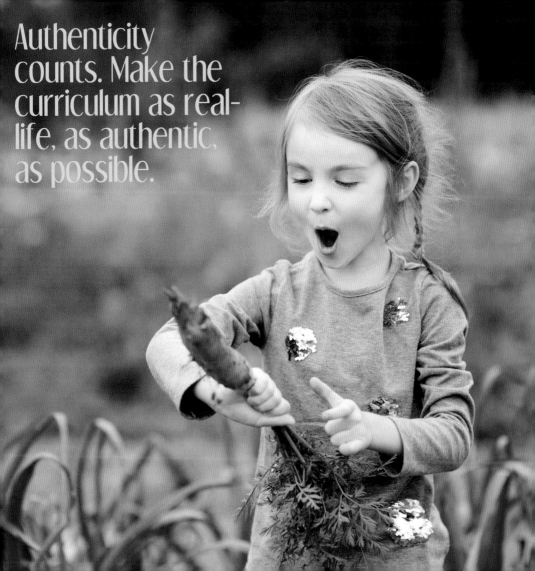

Authenticity counts. Make the curriculum as real-life, as authentic, as possible.

Never, EVER, set up an authentic doctor's office in the dramatic play area. Children will take off all of their clothes.

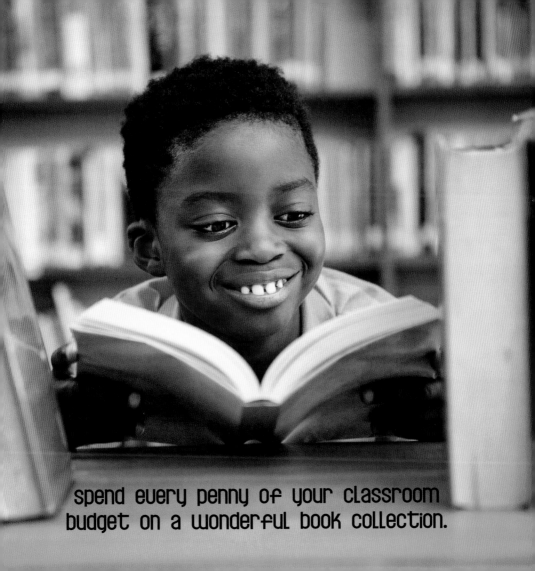

spend every penny of your classroom budget on a wonderful book collection.

Some great children's books should live in your classroom, not just in the library.

STUDY ANIMALS.
READ ABOUT THEM,
DRAW THEM, MAKE
THEIR SOUNDS AND
MOVEMENTS.

Never, EVER, buy a classroom pet as a part of your animal studies, unless you plan to pet-sit over all the holidays.

On the first day of school, declare that everything in the classroom belongs to everybody, but nobody can take anything home.

Buy tissues by the dozens.
Buy crayons and markers by the gross.

The more crayons and markers you have,
the fewer tissues you need.

Ask your family and friends to save magazines for art projects.

Never, **EVER** start the magazine art project until you have thrown out the swimsuit editions of sports magazines.

Never, **EVER** assign a child to be the big bad wolf.

Each child wants to be good.

You, on the other hand, can lead a convincing group growl for the big bad wolf.

ON SOME DAYS,
ALL CHILDREN
SEEM LIKE LITTLE
MONSTERS.

NEVER, EVER, CALL THEM LITTLE MONSTERS.
THEY MAY LIVE UP TO THE LABEL.

Never, EVER yell at a child.
Yellers always lose.

Curse in closets behind closed doors . . .

after you
make sure
no one is
hiding in
the closet.

SPEAK SOFTLY BUT ENTHUSIASTICALLY. IF YOU GET LOUD, THE CHILDREN GET LOUDER.

Keep your cool when all the little children around you are losing theirs.

Punishment is
for criminals.
Guidance is
for children.

Never, EVER nag.
Do brag—about the children.

Hug every child every day!

Let every child hug
you every day.

HUG YOUR ASSISTANT EVERY TIME YOU THINK HOW LIFE WOULD BE WITHOUT HER OR HIM.

Remember, secretaries and custodians
make life happier for teachers.
Hug them, too.

The hug at the end of the day is just as important as the greeting at the beginning of the day.

Never, EVER hold grudges. They don't mix with hugs.

Never, EVER say, "Sit Indian style."
Indians sit just like everyone else.
Say, "Sit cross-legged."

Have dolls of different races in your classroom.
Teddy bears are nonracial.

The best role model or courtesy is a courteous teacher.

Respect little people for what they can do today, not for what they are supposed to do next year.

You've heard old teachers say this adage:
"Never smile until Christmas."

Ignore that old adage.
If you don't smile, you'll
never make it to Christmas.

KEEP YOUR CAMERA HANDY.

AT PARENT MEETINGS, GIVE OUT PHOTOS OF CHILDREN ENGAGED IN CLASSROOM ACTIVITIES. IT INCREASES ATTENDANCE AT PARENT MEETINGS.

No child thinks he or she has time for time-out.

When you need a time-out, take a five-minute emergency break, and leave the room.

Avoid preachy tones.
You have a beautiful voice.

Few teachers do anything single-handedly.
There are many little helping hands.

Never, EVER, serve sugary snacks on rainy days.

BANANAS ARE FOR SNACKS NOT FOR GOING.

NEVER, EVER serve peanuts to young children.

Too many food allergies.

And, you don't want to pick peanuts out of nostrils and ears.

Teach children to suck up,
suck up, suck the milk up
through the straw,
and not to blow bubbles
down in the milk.

Never, EVER
"kiss it to make
it well."

You'll be
surprised at
what you are
asked to kiss.

Remember, no one wants to play the triangle in the rhythm band.

Everyone wants to play the drums.

And somehow, the kid with no rhythm always gets the cymbals.

Take turns with musical instruments. There is only so much out-of-rhythm noise you can take from the little kids' rhythm band.

Sing, dance, move—
it keeps you young and sane.

EXERCISE YOUR BODY AND YOUR MIND. STOOP DOWN AND LISTEN TO A CHILD TELL A FANTASY STORY.

Learn to make animal sounds.
Without animal sounds, you are not a
good preschool reader or singer.

Make silly faces.
Tell corny jokes.
Waddle like a duck.
Squawk like a hen.
Remember where
the fun begins.

Heredity versus environment is an irrelevant question for early childhood teachers. Teachers create learning environments regardless of one's heredity.

REMEMBER, YOUNG CHILDREN
LEARN THROUGH PLAY . . .

SO NEVER APOLOGIZE WHEN THE
CHILDREN TELL THEIR PARENTS,
"ALL WE DID WAS PLAY."

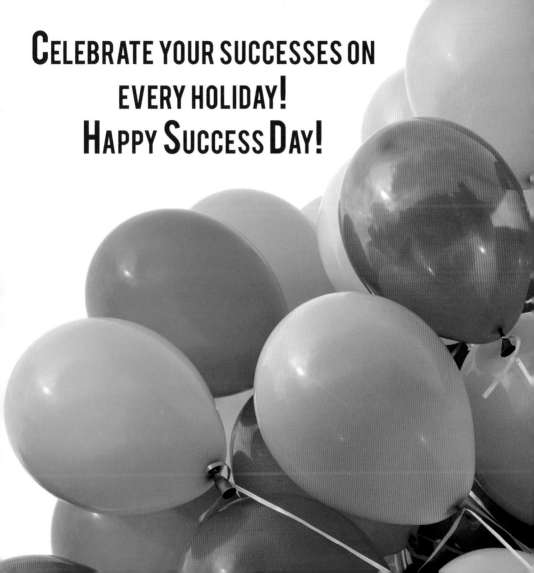

CELEBRATE YOUR SUCCESSES ON EVERY HOLIDAY! HAPPY SUCCESS DAY!

Have an after-school party every first Friday of the month.

No talking about children at after-school parties.

Look up to parents by seeing them through the eyes of their child.

KEEP PARENTS INFORMED, AND TAKE INFORMATION FROM PARENTS TO HEART.

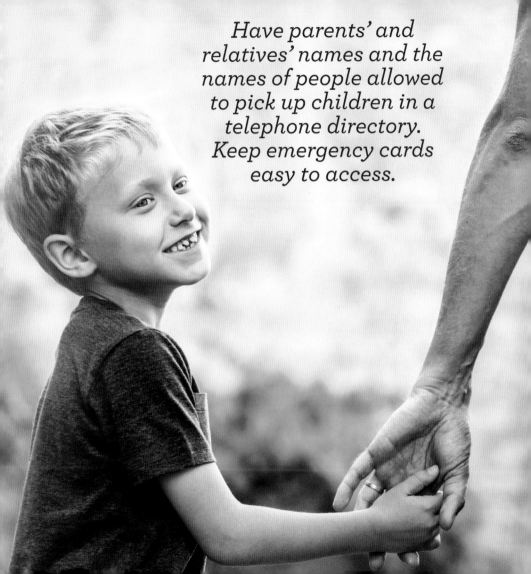

Have parents' and relatives' names and the names of people allowed to pick up children in a telephone directory. Keep emergency cards easy to access.

Never, EVER let someone pick up a child from your classroom unless he or she is listed on the permission card.

Keep a five-to-one ratio in conferences with parents. Say five wonderful statements about their child for every one concern you express.

Single parents, whether moms or dads, deserve double praise.

SUGGESTED READING:
ALL THE CLASSICS OF
CHILDREN'S LITERATURE.

Buy one great
children's book
per month to
build your own
collection.

PROVIDE PAINT SHIRTS, BUT PROMISE TO SEND CHILDREN HOME DIRTY.

Always put a
bit of liquid
soap in the
tempera paint
for quick
wash-ups.

Refrigerator-door art is displayed longer than most museum pieces.

ALWAYS HANG CHILDREN'S
ARTWORK AT EYE LEVEL—
THEIRS, NOT YOURS.

Never, EVER remove blocks from the classroom. They teach math, and they are monuments to creativity.

MATHEMATICS AND SCIENCE ARE A PART OF EVERY EARLY CHILDHOOD CLASSROOM.

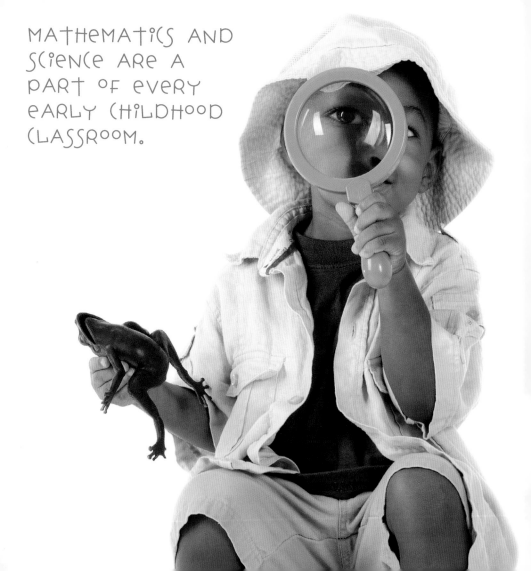

Never, EVER waste your money on gift-shop room decorations. Decorate the room with the children's art work.

Water tables and sand tables outlast any toy-store special.

The best field trips are walking field trips. Just going to the other side of the center or the school is an adventure for young children.

invite grandparents to volunteer for the walking field trips, not the off-campus ones. they have long memories. they remember their own children's field trips and will not volunteer.

Children love the color red, and they love to have books read to them.

ASK PARENTS TO DONATE A BOOK TO THE CLASSROOM LIBRARY TO CELEBRATE THEIR CHILD'S BIRTHDAY.

Never, EVER treat parents like guests. They are a part of your classroom family.

Invite grandparents to class
near the time for the school
scholarship fund-raiser.

Have five extra sets of clothes in the classroom . . .

four for the children
and one for you.

Accidents
happen.

Snot happens.

Ask parents for all the words their child uses for *urinate* and *defecate*.

Keep it simple.
Keep it clean.
Keep it confidential.

Don't buy markers that smell like fruit; the children eat them.

Never, EVER bring lip balm that
smells like fruit to your class
The children eat that, too

Plan a few mental
health days . . .

preferably in
February.
Everybody
needs a few
days off in
February.

Plan to get a cold . . .

You might as well
plan it; you'll get
one anyway.

Never, EVER take a nap at school—at least not until the children leave.

NEVER, EVER WEAR DANGLING EARRINGS. THEY ARE TOO TEMPTING FOR CHILDREN TO TUG.

Never, EVER bribe
children to behave,
except . . .

when the accreditation team is visiting.

unless, it is a musical, and the only songs
the children have to sing are the ones
they already know.

WEAR COMFORTABLE CLOTHING, OR YOU'LL BE TUGGING ALL DAY.

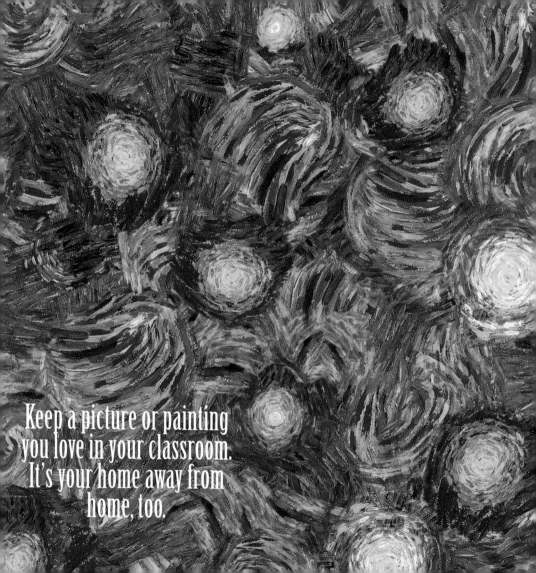

Keep a picture or painting
you love in your classroom.
It's your home away from
home, too.

*do small
things with
great
love*

Memorize some favorite quotes that inspire you.
Also, print them on small cards and keep them handy.
When times are tough, read a little card.

Ask your colleagues
for advice.
Try it and thank your lucky
stars you have colleagues
who are friends.

BE A FRIEND TO
YOUR TEACHER
COLLEAGUES,
NOT A CRITIC.

Take advice from the teachers who are the best. Ignore the rest.

Listen and learn. Learn to listen.

Clean up to help the custodian.

Make a list of ten complaints about the center's or the school's operation, but before you do anything with the list . . .

Make a second list of ten compliments about the center's or the school's operation.
Give the second list to the director.

Ask the custodian to test all cookie recipes.

Speak your mind, but remember the listener's heart.

Speak your heart,
but remember to
mind your words.

Stay a little too
sentimental.
Stay a little too sweet.
Stay a little too gentle.
Children are little, too.

Laugh a lot. It's a
great stress reliever.

Laugh a lot—with the children, not at them.

Look in the mirror and smile.
All children love real smiles,
but they can spot a fake.
Make it real.

Promises must be kept
in school and in life.

Teachers shop for fresh fruits and vegetables for snacks, and find fresh ideas to teach.

Take time to reflect
on your teaching.
Reflection requires
more than a mirror.

What is an early childhood teacher's favorite thing to do at a professional conference? Go to the exhibit hall and collect freebies for the classroom.

There is a core curriculum
for young children.
Experience is the core of
the child's knowledge.

Knowledge is unlimited.
Limit your quick answers
and help children find out.

Teachers are pretend discoverers. They must pretend not to know that yellow and blue make green. Every child deserves to know the thrill of discovering green.

Pot a few extra plants
to send home.
Little gardeners often
overwater their plants.

Carry on real conversations
with children.

Always read the note aloud to the child, before you pin it to his or her jacket.

Don't act grown up.
Be the grown-up.
There's already a whole
room full of children.

Teach good manners by example.
Teach good grammar by example.

Teachers know how to set limits
but limit limit-setting.

Teachers never, EVER feel the need to join a health club. Every day is a workout.

Learn to massage your feet.
Wait until after school to practice.

Tell everyone at a
party that you have
the most important
job—you teach.

Never, EVER say,
"I'm just a teacher."

Few people may recognize
your true value, but you
must truly value all people.

Hang out around influential people.

At dinner, don't ask them to pass the butter.
Ask them to pass the school bond.

Ask for the sunniest room.
Everyone is happier in the sunlight.

How can you spot the early childhood teacher?

She's the one with red tempera paint on her elbow.
He's the one who smells like school glue.
She's the one buying apple juice by the gallon.
He's the one who volunteers to sit on the floor at parties.

Roses require sunlight.
So do children.

Prune roses; cut them back.
Cut back on criticism.
Children don't need pruning.

Laugh a lot, smile a lot, cry a little.
Teaching is like that.

Too many teachers trust tests.

The younger the child, the less reliable the test results.

Besides, grades are best left to older classes.

portfolios are
not for stocks.
they are for
keeping samples
of children's
work.
they are the
best test
results.

Make a new year's resolution.
Resolve to operate a
peaceful classroom.

Pray for peace for all the little children and for all the teachers who teach them.

To share your best advice
for teachers of young
children, or to schedule
Shirley Raines for a
speech, please contact her
at sraines0445@gmail.com
or www.shirleyraines.com

Other Gryphon House books by Shirley C. Raines:

Story S-t-r-e-t-c-h-e-r-s: Activities to Expand Children's Favorite Books

More Story S-t-r-e-t-c-h-e-r-s: More Activities to Expand Children's Favorite Books

Story S-t-r-e-t-c-h-e-r-s for the Primary Grades: Activities to Expand Children's Favorite Books

450 More Story S-t-r-e-t-c-h-e-r-s for the Primary Grades: Activities to Expand Children's Favorite Books

Story S-t-r-e-c-h-e-r-s for Infants, Toddlers and Twos: Experiences, Activities, and Games for Popular Children's Books, with Karen Miller and Leah Curry-Rood

Story S-t-r-e-t-c-h-e-r-s for the Primary Grades: Activities to Expand Children's Favorite Books, revised edition, with Brian Scott Smith

Tell It Again! 1: Easy-to-Tell Stories with Activities for Young Children, with Rebecca Isbell

Tell It Again! 2: Easy-to-Tell Stories with Activities for Young Children, with Rebecca Isbell